PICTURE

POST

BRITAIN

PICTURE
POST
BRITAIN

Gavin Weightman

Picture research by
Philippa Lewis

TIGER BOOKS INTERNATIONAL
LONDON

This edition published in 1994 by
Tiger Books International PLC, London

First published in Great Britain in 1991
by Collins & Brown Limited
London House
Great Eastern Wharf
Parkgate Road
London SW11 4NQ

A CIP catalogue record for this book
is available from the British Library

ISBN 1-85501-585-4

Conceived, edited and designed by Collins & Brown Limited

Editorial Director: Gabrielle Townsend
Picture Research: Philippa Lewis
Art Director: Roger Bristow
Designed by: Gail Jones

Filmset by Servis Filmsetting Ltd, Manchester
Reproduction by Daylight, Singapore
Printed and bound in CHINA

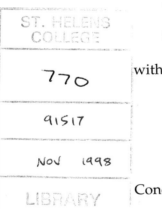
Half title: *Egg collector on top of cliffs near
Bampton, Flamborough Head, Yorks, July 1945*

Frontispiece: *A 'bedmaker', Cambridge,
June 1939*

Contents

INTRODUCTION

Flick through the pages of this collection of photographs from the legendary *Picture Post* magazine and, at a glance, nearly twenty years of a moving, heroic, comic and sometimes tragic episode in British history unfolds. None of the events, nor the ordinary, everyday stories, happened all that long ago: they are within the memories of many people alive today. But they have the feel of history, the raw material of an era well and truly gone, worked over and argued about by scholars.

Picture Post first appeared on the news stands on 1 October 1938, and was instantly accepted as an original eye on the world and on the social life of Britain. Its last issue came out on 1 June 1957, by which time it was long past its prime.

It had begun to deteriorate into a show-business magazine, struggling in the new age of television. Its exceptional photography, however, survived much longer than its journalistic excellence, and it continued to provide a uniquely compassionate vision of mundane things in the 1950s.

A great many questions are still asked about what really happened, what was true and what was myth, in this period of British history. It was an era which *Picture Post* not only chronicled: it played a very active part as well. Much cold water has been poured on the heroic view that prevailed just after the war: the stoicism of the Blitz, the miraculous performance of industry, the creation of the Welfare State and a more egalitarian society. It is said that Britain won the war—with American money and supplies—and lost the peace, when the weaknesses of its economy were revealed.

It is relatively easy to sustain such a cold and critical view of the nation's efforts when examining the evidence of production statistics, Government reports and so on. But, whatever errors there were, it is less easy to be unsympathetic when you re-examine, in the photographic record, the faces of those who lived through these years. On them are written the hopes, late in 1938, that war could be avoided; the fears of annihilation after war was declared in 1939, and then the anti-climax of the Phoney War; the horrors of the Blitz,

Picture Post *on sale at Paddington Station in 1942: the magazine, with its message of social reform, was widely read during the war.*

Fireguards on the roof of the House of Commons in November 1944, when the first and worst phase of the London Blitz ended and the bombers hit Coventry.

It was not all Blood, Sweat and Tears: on Blackpool beach in August 1942.

INTRODUCTION

and the determination to win a new way of life from the devastation; the disillusionment of the austere post-war years; and finally the fading of hopes for social revolution and the emergence of a new, more prosperous 'consumer society'.

Picture Post was a socially concerned magazine, and this pictorial history reflects to a large degree a central strand in the magazine's journalism from 1938 to 1957: the social transformation of Britain. *Picture Post* covered events world-wide, but it is the magazine's vivid images of the home front in war and peace that are selected here.

It is not in any way an objective history, for *Picture Post* itself inevitably took a political line on many subjects, and only a fraction of its reporting can be reproduced in one volume. The intention is to draw out subtle elements in the evolution of everyday life and to place them carefully in chronological order. It is a much easier exercise to pick out strong, and often famous, images from the magazine at different periods and juxtapose them. But that is much less revealing.

Picture Post only just caught the end of the Thirties, which were relatively prosperous years for the majority of the population. In fact, it was that very prosperity in the new middle-class suburbs that had been built between the wars that provided the magazine with its

readership—averaging one and a half million in its heyday—and its advertising. As a socially concerned publication, it often concentrated in its journalism on the poor and the unemployed, but never tediously or without humour.

In the first instance, it probably escaped a plodding piety because of the unusual background and the undoubted brilliance of its inventor and first editor. He hardly knew Britain at all and could see it with fresh eyes. Stefan Lorant was a Hungarian Jew who had gone to Germany in the 1920s where he worked in photography and film and became editor of a Munich paper that pioneered a new form of photo-journalism. In 1933 Hitler came to power and immediately arrested Lorant for criticizing the mistreatment of Jews by the Nazis. He was released after six months and came over to London via Paris to sell his book, *I Was Hitler's Prisoner*.

It did not take Lorant long to impress in Fleet Street. He began his own magazine, *Lilliput*, which had as a speciality the juxtaposition of unrelated images that resembled each other: Neville Chamberlain and a llama was a famous one. A wealthy young newspaper proprietor Edward Hulton, who had failed to get into Parliament as a Conservative, gave the anarchic Lorant the money to start a new magazine. Lorant's deputy was a young British journalist, Tom Hopkinson, who took

Forebodings of war in one of the most telling images from Picture Post. *A nun tries on her gas mask in May 1939.*

A home in the Gorbals, Glasgow's notorious slum, in 1948, the year the modern Welfare State was founded.

over as editor when Lorant decided to settle in America in 1940. Hopkinson was bequeathed the brilliant photographers Lorant had brought with him from Germany, and brought in the home-grown talents of Bert Hardy and Humphrey Spender, among others.

The picture of life in Britain these photographers began to present was unusually vivid for a number of reasons. Firstly, Hopkinson—like the German photo-journalists—had a political and emotional interest in 'ordinary working people'. He was friendly with Tom Harrisson, co-founder of that extraordinary organization Mass Observation, which was set up in 1937 to study the minutiae of everyday life. They were rather like a team of anthropologists observing an unknown tribe. Harrisson and Mass Observation provided a good number of *Picture Post* stories.

A second reason for the magazine's uniqueness was the insistence that journalist and photographer work on a story together. It rejected the Fleet Street practice of treating the man with the camera as an inferior being. Working together, photographer and reporter got much deeper into things. Lastly, the magazine was prepared to run a sequence of pictures which together told a story. This created wonderful new opportunities for photo-graphers like Bert Hardy who felt cramped by the one-shot style of Fleet Street presentation.

There is, arguably, a further reason for the special quality of *Picture Post*: the editorial freedom the owner, Edward Hulton, gave to its staff. Though a 'natural' Conservative, Hulton was caught up in the general enthusiasm for reform which infected a wide spectrum of Establishment opinion from the Thirties until the Fifties; and by 1945 he was behind Labour. He wrote for *Picture Post* himself, but his were dull contributions to such a vibrant magazine. Mostly he let the staff get on with it, until he fell out with Hopkinson in 1950.

Hopkinson told a story which nicely illustrates Lorant's relationship with his patron. As the first-ever issue was being put together, and the threat of war with Germany was getting closer, Hulton suggested to Hopkinson that there should be a battleship on the cover. Worried that this might put people off, Hopkinson mentioned the idea to Lorant, and suggested that in his own opinion they would do better with a girl. 'There will be two girls,' said Lorant. And there were, though who they are nobody seems to have discovered. It was an agency picture, of two girls leaping in the air, somewhere in the world.

A Liverpool street scene in 1954 when Britain was becoming affluent and leaving behind rationing, austerity and war-time idealism.

A survival of rural Britain which disappeared almost completely after the war. Crofters cutting hay on the Isle of Lewis in 1955.

INTRODUCTION

By 1950, Hulton was opposed to the Labour Government and refused to publish a story written by James Cameron and photographed by Bert Hardy on the mistreatment of prisoners of war by South Koreans. Hopkinson was sacked, and thereafter a series of editors attended the downward trend of journalistic standards, and ultimately sales figures, until *Picture Post*'s demise.

In retrospect, 1957 was a fitting time for it to go, for a great many of the enthusiasms which had been a large part of its appeal in the Thirties and Forties had begun to fade by the mid-1950s. All that faith in planning for a better future, jobs for all, the clearance of slums, the banishment of all kinds of hardship and disease had been shaken by the years of austerity at the end of the war. Television, which *Picture Post* had thought would not catch on, achieved its first mass audience for the Coronation in 1953; and the arrival of commercial stations in 1955 provided new and fierce competition for a magazine celebrated for its dazzling visual imagery.

We look back on these years now after more than a decade of what became known as Thatcherism. In essence, this new mood—which pre-dated Margaret Thatcher's first year as Prime Minister in 1979—was a rejection of all that *Picture Post* stood for in social affairs.

The Welfare State it campaigned for during the war was looking tattered and worn, the intellectuals it marshalled to make the case for a New Britain, discredited as misguided do-gooders. This change in the prevailing philosophy, as well as the undoubted rise in living standards for the majority which began in the mid-1950s, emphasizes how old-fashioned the world of *Picture Post* appears from the perspective of the 1990s.

The story of *Picture Post Britain* begins back in October 1938, and is taken in its first phase up to September 1940 when the bombing of London began in earnest. From the first days of the Blitz until the end of the war there was a determination to plan for a better future: that was phase two, which ended with the war and the remarkable victory for Labour (its first-ever taste of real power), and the summary dismissal of the war hero Churchill. A third phase began with Labour's attempt to fulfil the promises for a Welfare State while struggling to survive financially. Finally, there is the dismissal of Labour in 1951, disillusionment with the years of austerity and the first glimpses of an affluent future. The finale is provided by Harold Macmillan with his celebrated pronouncement: 'You've never had it so good.'

The London to Dover cycle race in Coronation year, 1953.

One of the last of Picture Post's *famous documentary features, published in 1955. Photographer Slim Hewitt went out with the trawlermen of Fleetwood.*

The affluent worker's home in 1957, the year of 'You've never had it so good'. This car worker was, in fact, made redundant. Picture Post *killed the story, and ceased publication a few months later in June 1957.*

DOING THE LAMBETH WALK

1938–1939

WHEN THE FIRST ISSUE of *Picture Post* appeared, 80 pages long, price 3d, on 1 October 1938, it was not at all certain that in less than a year Britain would once again be at war. Elaborate civil defence plans were being laid, and 38 million gas masks had been issued to regional centres. In August of that year the newly formed Mass Observation, a pioneer of market research and opinion polling, had found about a third of the population expected war, but most of them thought it was a long way off.

At the same time there were fearful predictions about the devastation bombing would bring. All the experts agreed on this, and the first bombardment the people of Britain had to suffer was an onslaught of horrifying statistics: there were predictions of 20,000 dead in a single raid on London, and 20 million square feet of timber a month needed for coffins. There was a belief that ordinary people could not cope with this kind of Armaggedon, that they would panic and civil order would break down. It was a popular military theory that this is how wars would be fought—subduing the enemy civilians and destroying the productive capacity of the nation. According to Mass Observation's interviews and their team of informants who kept diaries, remarkably little notice was taken of all this. There was not much anybody could do anyway to avert such a catastrophe. So they went on living their lives.

Nevertheless, there was great jubilation at the hopes raised for peace when Neville Chamberlain returned from Munich brandishing his peace agreement with Hitler. *Picture Post* just missed it for their first issue, but carried the story on 8 October. How sad it is now to be reminded of the cheering crowds who gathered outside 10 Downing Street that night to hear the Prime Minister speak the fateful words: 'I believe it is peace for our time.'

History has made Chamberlain's apparent optimism laughable and tragic. In fact, he had many misgivings, and he was not alone in his desperate desire for peace. He was applauded, and many who were wise after the event voted for him.

There were no general elections between 1935 and 1945, and the country was therefore not tested on its views on major domestic issues, the most pressing of which between the wars was unemployment. The worst of the Depression was over, but there were still two million unemployed. As it turned out, this was one problem the war was about to solve, for the gearing up of the economy for the production of weapons, and then the conscription of four and a half million men into the forces mopped up the entire working population. For the great majority of the people who were in work

War is still a long way off in February 1938 as Liverpool police test their gas masks—to the amusement of local children.

this was a period of modest but very real prosperity, especially in the south of England. While the old industries were suffering, and the ship-building town of Jarrow on Tyneside registered 75 per cent of its men out of work, London was a boom town. It seemed to be becoming in a way American, with neon-lit factories springing up along the Great West Road.

In 1938, while the doomsters were prophesying the 'destruction of civilization' and preparing for a nationwide panic, the people themselves were caught up in a euphoric craze which swept the dance halls. It was a song-and-dance routine called 'The Lambeth Walk'. Everybody did it—in posh West End clubs, in country halls, even down the Lambeth Walk itself in South London.

It was a bit of nonsense that originated in a show called *Me and My Gal*, in which an ordinary couple working in a grand house discover they have inherited a lot of money. The Lambeth Walk on stage was performed by Lupino Lane. Naturally, *Picture Post* despatched one team to have a look at the real Lambeth Walk with its eel and pie shops and typically down-at-heel but chirpy cockney culture, and another—the redoubtable Mass Observation—to make sense of this strange outburst of exuberance. If you could understand this, thought Tom Harrisson, the investigator, you might make sense of a modern democracy. One explanation for the popularity of the Lambeth Walk is that there was a desire unconsciously to celebrate the passing of the old world of Victorian poverty in the 1930s, and a nostalgia for it. That does not explain why it swept through Paris, New York and Prague and was doing well in Nazi Germany until it was banned for being 'too negroid'.

This was an age of mass entertainment which provided for very large numbers of people previously undreamed-of luxury, exemplified by the great dance halls, and the cinema. These Picture Palaces were in reality just *that* in the Thirties when home comforts were fewer.

The social issues and pastimes of the Thirties are in one way quite familiar, in another quaintly out-of-date. A new and very characteristic entertainment of the inter-war years was greyhound racing, or 'The Dogs'. The first of these tracks on which competing greyhounds chased an electric hare was opened in 1926, and by 1931 it was estimated there were 18 million 'attendances'. London had seventeen tracks. In those days it was illegal to bet 'off course' on horses or dogs, but the greyhound tracks were much more accessible to gamblers in town and took maybe a tenth of the money that went on betting in an era with a mania for gambling. *Picture Post*, of course, sent a reporter-photographer team to watch.

In its choice of other subjects worthy of closer scrutiny it was governed, as were all magazines, by the possibilities for striking visual imagery. A now famous picture is that of the girl on the roller-coaster at Southend funfair, her skirt flying and suspenders showing. The caption read: 'War cares blown away.' In contrast to this fantasy image, there is the wonderful photo-feature on the National Spinsters Pension Association—a real Thirties period piece.

The Association was founded by Miss Florence White, owner of a small sweet shop in Bradford who felt it was a great injustice that widows could have pensions but not women who had never married. Though marriage rates had been rising since the

Neville Chamberlain leaving No. 10 for the House: his secretary carried the gas mask.

Winston Churchill at Blenheim in 1939, still in the political wilderness.

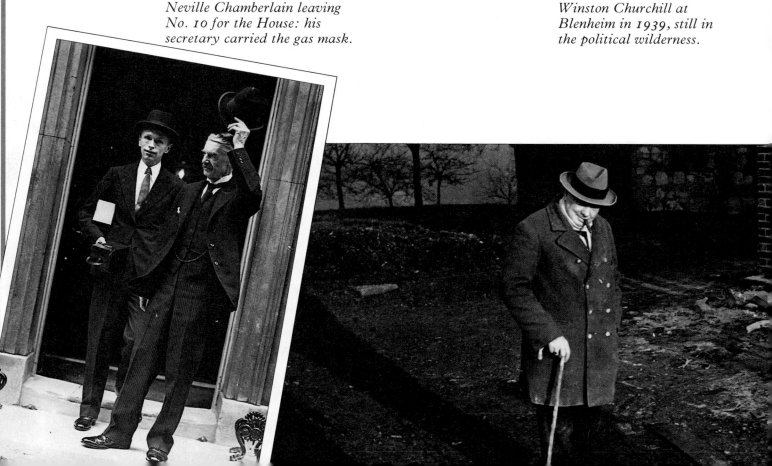

1920s—that is, more women of each generation were married at progressively younger ages—there were still many spinsters. A popular myth is that they remained single because their would-be husbands were slaughtered in the Great War. But there were much more important reasons. Firstly, it was the social custom from the late Victorian period for a large proportion (about a quarter) of women to remain unmarried. You wed only if you had the money to do so, and quite late in life. There was also an imbalance of women over men chiefly because of the mass emigration before the Great War.

At the same time, the early steps towards a Welfare State, including the granting of old-age pensions from 1909, excluded many people. Spinsters got a raw deal. Those who worked and paid contributions lost their pension if they had to give up their jobs before retirement age; and if they did not work— many cared for relatives—they had no pension. 'The young and wise,' Miss White was quoted as saying, 'get into the protected industry of marriage.'

The impending war was to have a remarkable influence on social attitudes and was to open the eyes of the well-to-do to a world of hardship and poverty they knew little about. Buckingham Palace and Mayfair were bombed and the evacuation of ragged children from the crumbling city centres brought the reality of poverty to public attention more forcibly than any of the social surveys of the 1930s.

War was declared on Sunday 3 September 1939 when Hitler failed to respond to an 11 a.m. deadline set by Chamberlain. A large part of the population heard the Prime Minister's declaration on the radio, and later the same day all over the country air-raid sirens were sounded. People ran this way and that, taking cover where they could. They waited, and nothing happened. The all clear sounded, and everyone emerged from under tables, from ditches, from hastily constructed shelters.

It was a long wait before the bombardment started, and many of those who had fled London in the days after the first sirens were sounded drifted back to the towns. When Mass Observation polled a small sample of Londoners in the winter of 1939, half did not think there would be any bombing. The first enemy bomb fell, by accident—a side-effect of a raid on shipping at Scapa Flow—on 16 March 1940, killing a cottager at Bridge of Waith in Scotland. There were one or two other raids, but it was a year before Germany made a determined attempt to subdue the civilian population of Britain.

What seemed more likely, and what was in fact the first intention of Hitler, was invasion. The defeated troops of the British Expeditionary force limped back across the Channel from Dunkirk in May and June. Then the air attacks, which had concentrated on shipping, were aimed at the Royal Air Force at its bases in East Anglia. If the Luftwaffe could smash Britain's air power it could easily cross the Channel. What became known as the Battle of Britain began, with aerial dog fights witnessed by many civilians on the ground. It was a close-fought battle but the Luftwaffe began to lose a great many aircraft. In frustration, it seems, Hitler turned his bombers on London—a tactic which many have subsequently regarded as a serious military error. Whether or not it was that, the decision had a momentous influence on the subsequent evolution of British history.

Fashionable ladies in Grosvenor Street, Mayfair, 1939.

An eel and pie saloon in Lambeth, 1938.

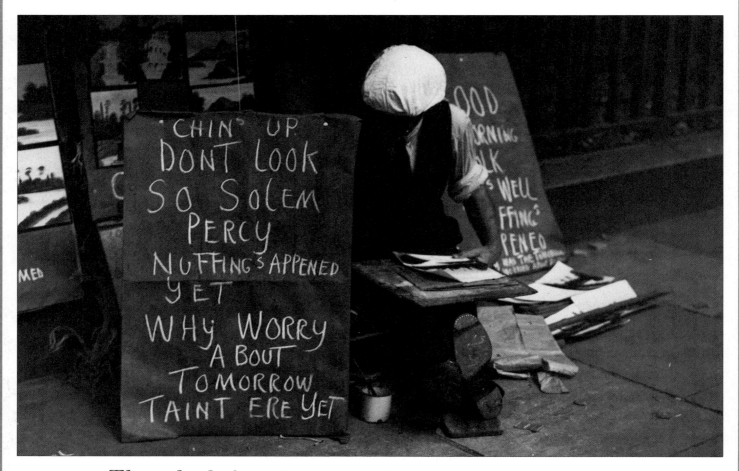

The calm before the storm: Britain awaits its fate in the summer of 1939 with characteristic humour and phlegm . . .

In May 1939 men began to sign on for
military training in labour exchanges (right).
An immediate effect of the preparation for
war was work and pay for the unemployed,
in the army or the armaments industry.
Though the worst of the Depression was over
by 1939, there were still two million out of
work (above and below). A year later,
unemployment had disappeared altogether.

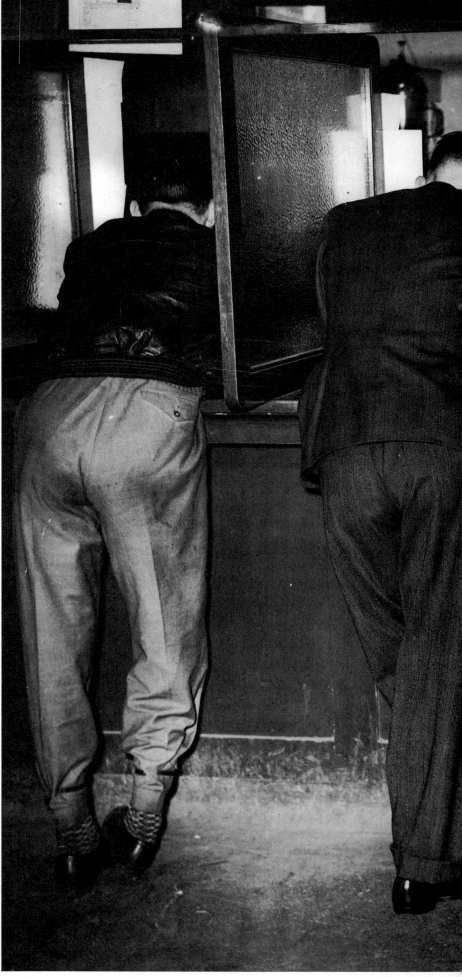

PICTURE POST BRITAIN

*Doing the song-and-dance routine the Lambeth Walk
was all the rage in 1938 and 1939. It was a hit with all
social classes, and swept the world (below). But what
did it mean? Typically,* Picture Post *puzzled over the
significance of this strange celebration of cockney
culture, providing a portrait (opposite, above and
below) of the poor but jolly district of south London
which gave its name to the dance hall craze.*

Factory girls began to dress like American film stars in the Thirties—a prosperous time for those in work, in which the dance hall and dance band provided mass entertainment. Two images here from Wigan, which George Orwell had portrayed so gloomily: workers passing a cinema poster outside the factory (below); *and taking to the dance floor* (left).
(Opposite) *A classic Thirties image from a 1939* Picture Post *feature on the life of a barmaid.*

(Overleaf) *Another side of British life— a vicarage garden party in September 1939.*

Gambling on greyhounds was one of the fads of the 1930s. The first stadiums, in which the dogs chased an electric hare, were opened in 1926. Off-course betting was then illegal, and the new stadiums, built in towns, gave the punters a legal way of losing their money which was much more accessible than horse-racing. The working man with his muzzled dogs became a classic urban image (below, Glasgow 1939). The other pictures are from a 1938 Picture Post feature: 'Dogs That Carry Money.'

Two contrasting images of life's ups and downs for women in the 1930s—the protesting spinster and the frolicking girl on a roller coaster at Southend funfair.

Though there had been terrible warnings about what Hitler's bombers would do to London; though a year earlier Chamberlain had been cheered when he returned from Munich with his peace agreement; though nobody wanted war—when it came it was greeted with a strange equanimity. A week before the declaration of war, crowds await news in Downing Street (left). On the fateful day, 3 September, crowds watch Big Ben strike the hour of ultimatum (below). The King reads the declaration of war not only to Britain but to the whole of the Empire (opposite above). The following day two soldiers study the King's Proclamation posted at the Duke of York's steps in London (opposite below).

*War has begun, preparations have been made—
but nothing happens on the Home Front for
another year.*

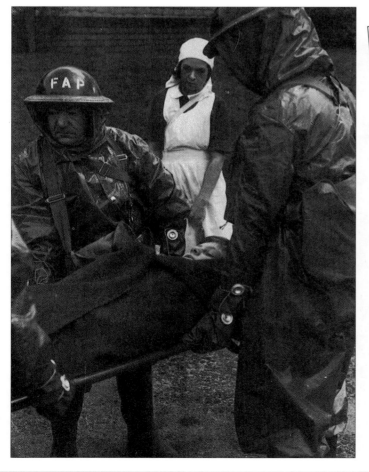

The battlefront moved closer to home in the spring of 1940, when the British Expeditionary Force had to retreat, escaping across the Channel from Dunkirk. Though invasion was expected at any time, there was great relief that so many of the men had got back safely. As the trains brought the soldiers back from the coast they were given an impromptu welcome by people living along the tracks (above) and some comfort from well-wishers at the stations (left and opposite). For the time being, their war was over—the real fight would be in the air.

'The Few'—the airmen who foiled Hitler's plans
to win air superiority early in the war to clear
the way for invasion. They won the Battle of
Britain—but the war had only just begun.

BLOOD, SWEAT AND TEARS

1939–1945

WHEN WINSTON CHURCHILL BECAME Prime Minster after Chamberlain's resignation in May 1940 he offered the nation in his first Commons speech only 'blood, sweat and tears'. Nobody knew quite what that meant until the Blitz began on 7 September, a Saturday in 1940. This report on 'Black Saturday', by an observer in Stepney, in London's East End, went into the Mass Observation files:

> 'At 8.15 p.m. a colossal crash, as if the whole street was collapsing; the shelter itself is shaking. Immediately, an A.R.P. [Air Raid Precautions] helper, a nurse, begins singing lustily, in an attempt to drown out the noise—"Roll out the barrel . . .!"—while Mrs S., wife of a dyer and cleaner screams: "My house! It come on my house! My house is blown to bits!" As the bombing continues a man shouts at the A.R.P. helper who is still trying to get people to sing: "Shut your bleedin' row!"'

The first days of the Blitz were a terrible trauma, and the stalwart spirit of the people did not at first assert itself. They had to get used to being bombed every night. In his invaluable account of the reality of those nights, *Living through the Blitz*, based on Mass Observation reports and his own experiences, Tom Harrisson noted that the weeping of women became less common in the shelters as the grim, blacked-out nights wore on. Those who chose to stay in London were perhaps self-selected for their toughness.

A new evacuation began. Many people from Stepney headed for Epping Forest; a nightly trek to the West End of London and the tube stations began for those East Enders who returned to their homes—or the ruins of them—during the day. At first, the Government closed the Underground stations, fearing a 'shelter mentality' would develop and nobody would come out of their hiding place to work. But public pressure won, and each night families took up their area of a platform claimed by squatters' rights.

From the very first, the Blitz levelled not only large areas of London but social divisions as well. In the wealthier areas—if the inhabitants had not fled to America or the country—maidservants settled down for the night in the same cellar as their employers. A second evacuation of children, initially from London's East End, revealed once again the poverty and ill-health that many suffered.

The bombing not only of London, but of Coventry, Manchester, Birmingham and other cities, was a decisive phase of the war,

A typical propaganda image of the Blitz in London: a milkman, white as snow, his full crate untouched, emerges mysteriously from the ruins of a bombed street. Where has he come from? Where is he going? Only the photographer knows.

steeling the determination to fight back. It was equally decisive in setting light to a fuse that had burned slowly in the Thirties: the demand for social reform. The military strategists were utterly wrong. You could not subdue a nation by bombing civilians, whether they were Londoners or Berliners. Germans suffered, in the end, far harsher treatment but did not submit. What the Blitz did do was to shape future social policy. As A. J. P. Taylor put it in *English History 1914–45*: 'The Luftwaffe was a powerful missionary for the Welfare State.'

A schism opened in the hearts and minds of the British people. Winston Churchill was greatly admired, even idolized, as the war dog. Nearly everyone tried to catch his theatrical performances on radio—far more, according to Mass Observation, than listened to the hapless King George VI, who stammered and was 'dull'. *Picture Post* ran a wonderful sequence of photographs on 'Listening to Churchill'.

But while there was great confidence in Churchill as a war leader, a sense grew stronger and stronger that he was not in sympathy with what people hoped for and dreamed of when the war was over. Victory was his single aim: the clamour for social reform he tried to suppress, as unrealistic.

Though people even in the Blitzed areas were able to continue their daily lives with remarkable equanimity, a great many social problems had to be dealt with immediately. One of the most pressing was homelessness, and in surveys later in the war it was new housing that the majority put at the top of their list of hoped-for peacetime welfare. To deal with the casualties of bombing, the hospitals had been organized into a single administration, bringing together those run by local authorities and the independent voluntary hospitals. Not only soldiers, but civilians who were now in the front line had to be offered medical care.

So the necessities of war in these and many other spheres appeared to provide a practical demonstration of the virtues of what social reformers had been demanding before the war. And they began to make their point early on. On 4 January 1941, in the middle of the Blitz, *Picture Post* published a special issue on *A Plan for Britain*. Distinguished contributors put forward their proposals for a new society: 'Work for All', 'Health for All' and so on. It was a blueprint for what became known as the Welfare State. An editorial in that issue wrung its hands:

> '. . . Our plan for a new Britain is not something outside the war, or something *after* the war. It is an essential part of our war aims. It is, indeed, our most positive war aim. The new Britain is the country we are fighting for.'

Not only civilians but also the millions serving in the Forces were heartened by this promise of a better future. Popular acclaim for such plans reached a peak with the publication on 1 December 1942 of the Beveridge Report. This was one of the most extraordinary episodes in the war, which has recently been attacked as a Utopian folly. Britain should have been looking to modernize its industry rather than improve its social services. For the mass of ordinary people living through the war, however, the promise of a more just society (as well as the relative prosperity they enjoyed because of the demands war made on industry) was undoubtedly real and important. *Picture Post* was an ardent supporter of Beveridge.

One of the great problems of morale in wartime is not terror or extreme excitement, but boredom. The captive audience of millions of troops, most of whom were confined to Britain between Dunkirk and D-Day four years later, provided plenty of scope for discussion and education. The social levelling included the despatch of artists to the heart of grimy, cultureless industry, with *Picture Post* following

William Beveridge at the home of Picture Post *owner Edward Hulton.*

Stanley Spencer as war artist on Clydeside, 1943.

The artistic 'pin-up' Jury.

BLOOD, SWEAT AND TEARS

hotfoot. They produced a piece on the painter Stanley Spencer among the shipyard workers of Clydeside. This inspired the suggestion that the pin-up girl pictures that troops got chiefly from American cinema magazines might be replaced by specially commissioned artistic nudes. This was a fine chance for Mass Observation to conduct a study for *Picture Post*. A sample of troops was asked to rate a dozen studies of women, ranging from the *Daily Mirror*'s strip cartoon heroine, *Jane*, to a fifteenth-century study by Roger van der Weyden. The old master's work crashed to bottom place with 'minus 24 votes'; the winner was a lovely lady photographed stark naked on a rock, her hair blowing in the breeze.

By the middle of 1941, Hitler had called the Luftwaffe away from Britain. For a long period the bombing stopped, and terror did not return until the V1 and V2 rockets fell on London. There was still hardship, with rationing and homelessness, but a kind of normality returned. For a great many people, the war brought a relative prosperity. Women's fashions continued to evolve, while women donned overalls and worked during the day in factories. Everyone had to knuckle down: at Buckingham Palace, where the King and Queen insisted on staying, imported American spam was served on the royal table. George VI, a reluctant king, did his duty and people respected him for it, while feeling rather sorry for him with his speech impediment.

At the railway stations women met and waved goodbye to their men. The brunt of the fighting before 1944 was borne by the bombers which tried to destroy German morale—with as little success as the Luftwaffe had in Britain—and by the navy which protected essential supplies in the Atlantic. Much of the army was at home, preparing to invade Europe.

Germany was now outgunned, with Americans joining the Allies in the war; and though Japan inflicted heavy defeats on the British forces, there was a growing confidence that victory would be assured, in time. The greatest problem was keeping the nation supplied with food and essential materials. Amongst the bravest on this home front were the fishermen and those who manned the mine-sweepers. Patriotic gardening—'Digging for Victory', as it was called—was a pleasant pastime. The Home Guard—later immortalized in the television series *Dad's Army*—had been hastily assembled to repel invasion. By 1942 it had 1,600,000 men trained up, but the threat of invasion had gone away.

For those back home, there was, in fact, plenty of free time to be enjoyed in a most peculiar, unreal, kind of atmosphere—everyone had to keep everyone else happy. People even went on holiday, though most of the big seaside resorts had been commandeered for army accommodation. Writing of the Second World War in the round, A. J. P. Taylor judged it 'a brief period in which the English people felt they belonged to a truly democratic community'.

A great many people wanted that atmosphere to be sustained when the war was over, and for the lessons of social welfare to be learned. By 1944, the Government had produced a series of White Papers with plans for a health service, for full employment, and for social security. In that year a new Education Act was passed. It was, in the words of Beveridge, going to be 'A people's war for a people's peace'.

The re-invasion of Europe by the Allies—D-Day—began on 6 June 1944. As the forces swept through France, fighting hard all the way and greeted as liberators, a sigh of relief was heard in Britain. Five days later, the flying bombs, Hitler's secret weapon, began to fall on London, and the evacuation began again. But on the south and east coasts, people were allowed back on the beaches, which had been the front line of defence, to relax. It was nearly another year before Germany surrendered, but the main theatre of war was now in Europe.

A pram full of wartime salmon netted on the River Dee.

The beginning of the end for Hitler: Normandy, 1944.

BLOOD, SWEAT AND TEARS

The people's war began in September 1940 with the first of the air raids. From then on, civilians were in the front line and had to be treated by authority with the same respect as fighting forces. Although London took the brunt of the first onslaught, other towns, such as Coventry and Plymouth, were badly hit as well. A parson in the severely hit East End of London (opposite above left); fighting the fires after a raid on Portsmouth (opposite above right); a hole blown in London suburbs still gaping in 1944 (opposite below). Devastation in the City of London (above); and Winston Churchill (below) visiting the ruins of the Free Trade Hall in Manchester, which was bombed early in 1941.

The evacuation of children from cities to the countryside, and sometimes abroad, was one of the most heart-rending consequences of the Blitz. After the early evacuations at the beginning of the war, many children returned home as no bombs had fallen, only to be sent out of town again soon. Socially, this exodus of many poor children had an enormous impact, revealing as it did the extent and consequences of poverty. This three-month-old baby and her mother are preparing to leave for Australia in August 1940, along with 483 other children (right). (Below) The anguish of mothers who have waved their children goodbye. (Opposite) Brave smiles from two youngsters leaving London from Paddington Station in 1942.

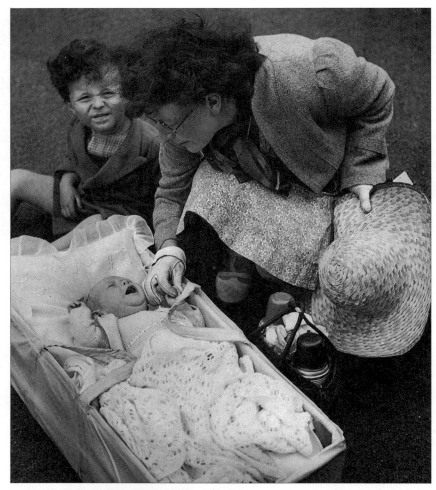

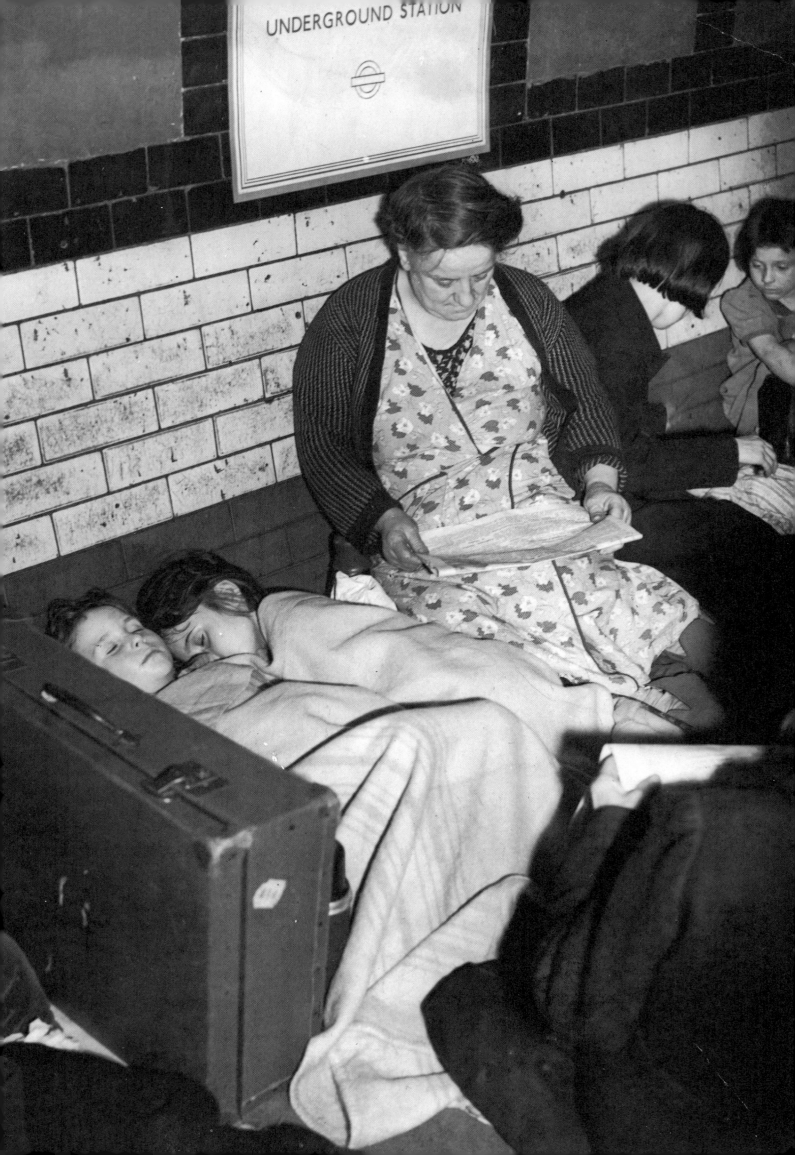

Nobody knew when the Blitz began how Londoners would react. There was a fear that if they were allowed into deep shelters—especially the Underground—they would stay there and refuse to come out. But the military theorists who thought you could win wars by bombing civilians into submission misjudged human nature. A shelter culture arose, families claimed their own spot on the platform (opposite), and the fashionable bedded down in the basements of hotels and clubs (right). Singing was encouraged to maintain morale (above), and artists entertained the civilians in the front line.

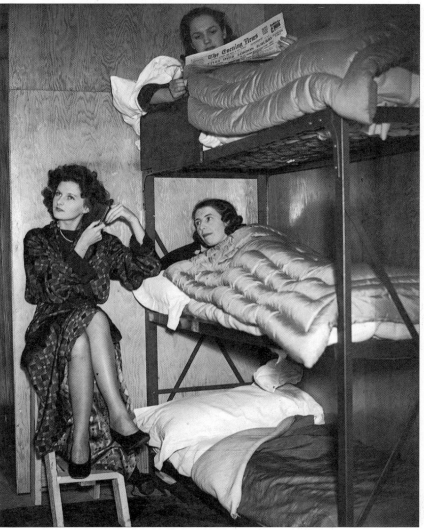

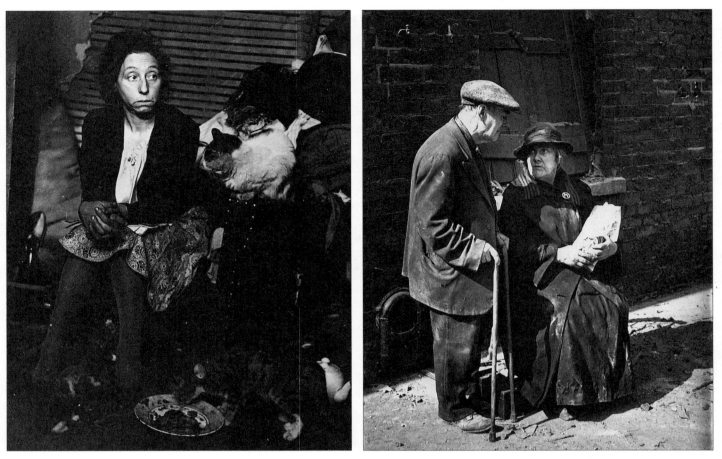

Many Londoners emerged safely from their bomb shelters only to discover their homes had been reduced to rubble in the night.

BLOOD, SWEAT AND TEARS

Whenever Winston Churchill made one of his speeches on radio the country stopped to listen, wherever they were at the time. Though there was, from early in the war, a rising tide of belief that what was being fought for was a better, fairer Britain as well as the defeat of Hitler, Churchill was cautious about making promises. Mostly he offered 'Blood, Sweat and Tears' and confidence in eventual victory.

*The exceptional demands of war become routine
. . . rationing, gas mask rehearsals, security,
digging for victory.*

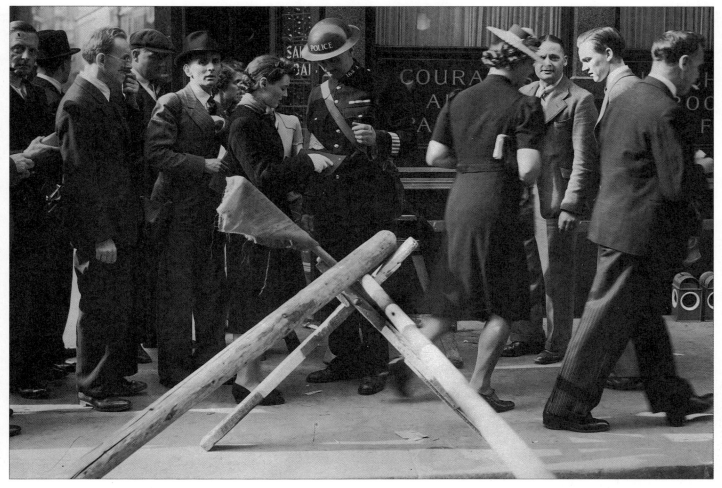

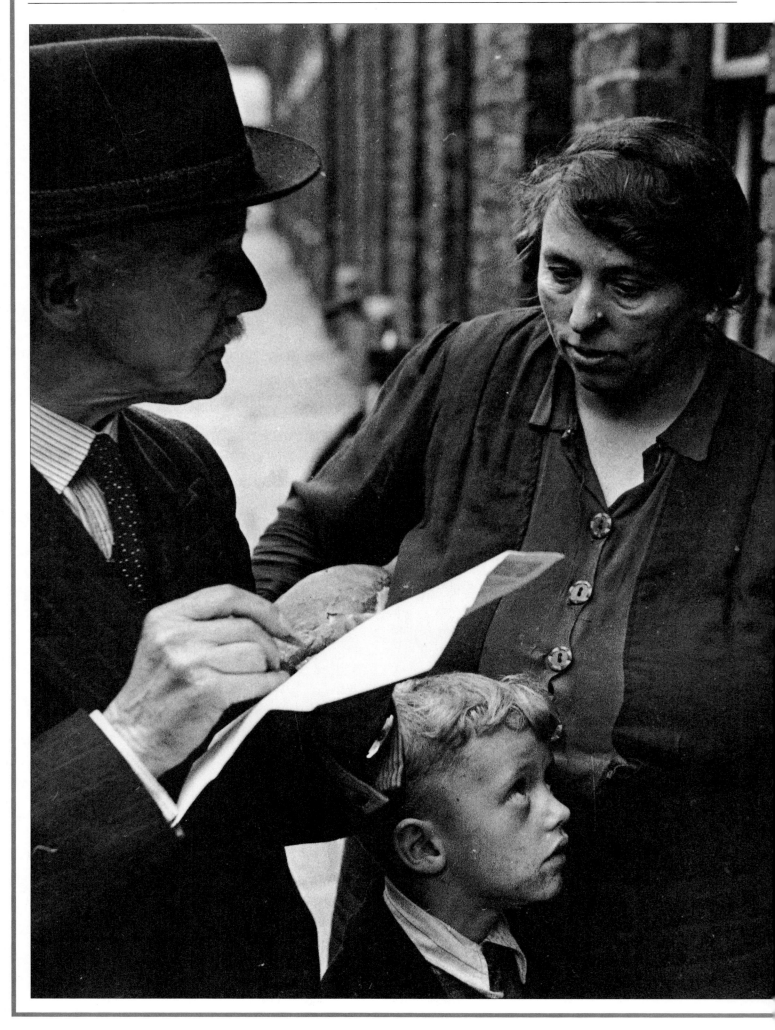

From as early as 1941 social reformers were demanding that the practice of running social and health services in wartime should be continued in the peace. Picture Post was in the vanguard of the desire to create a New Britain from the ruins of the war. Public opinion was canvassed on the possibility of a National Health Service. Approval was not universal but such socialist ideas gained in acceptabilty during the war, when more and more people became accustomed to the Government getting involved in almost every aspect of their lives.

There was still a discussion going on about whether women should wear trousers, although the war machine was being 'manned' by women. Femininity underwent some fundamental, though not necessarily permanent, changes during the war. Those who wanted to remain 'traditional' had to contend with clothes rationing and 'make do and mend'. Magazines like Picture Post regularly ran features on how to make fashionable clothes out of old dusters.

Of great symbolic importance, and part of the
social levelling of wartime experience, was the
acceptance by the Royal Family that they too
would have to tighten their belts and live on
rations. The King and Queen refused to leave
London during the Blitz and toured the bombed
areas. (Above) A war working party in
Buckingham Palace. (Below) The King inspecting
bomb damage in Lambeth. (Right) The Royal
Party watching a football match between England
and Scotland in 1944. Field Marshal
Montgomery is on the far right.

*'We'll meet again', the hope of everyone at the
wartime railway stations.*

Between the retreat from Dunkirk in 1940 and D-Day in 1944, a large part of the British Army was encamped in Britain, while the air force tried to bomb Germany into submission. Though the cracking of the Luftwaffe system of direction-finding and the great advances in the use of radar led to the success of the war in the air, British and American bombers were no more able to break the spirit of the Germans than the Luftwaffe was to subdue London.

(Overleaf) Preparations in the English countryside in 1941 for the eventual re-invasion of Europe.

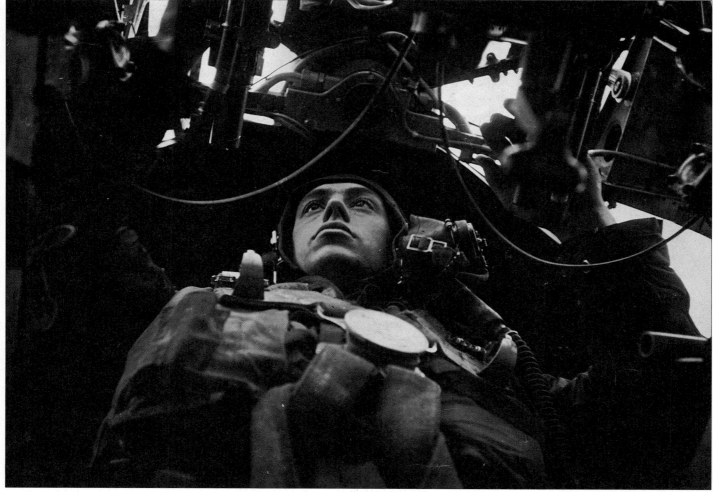

*Keeping Britain's lifeline afloat: barrage
balloons and minesweepers protecting the coast.*

Digging and pigging for victory. Britain imported the bulk of its food before the war, and though supplies still came in from abroad the nation had to use its ingenuity to produce more at home. Fire fighters herd their porkers, fed on dustbin leftovers, in the ruins of Lincoln's Inn, London (left), while the ornamental gardens by the Albert Memorial were turned into allotments (above).

*The real Dad's Army—the Home Guard
prepares to repel the invasion that never came.*

Entertaining the troops: (opposite) *Vera Lynn;* (above) *stars at a bomber station;* (below top) *a new chorus line for a wartime West End show;* (below bottom) *getting ready for the show in a Nissen hut changing room;* (right) *Tommy Trinder.*

With American help, the war was almost won . . .

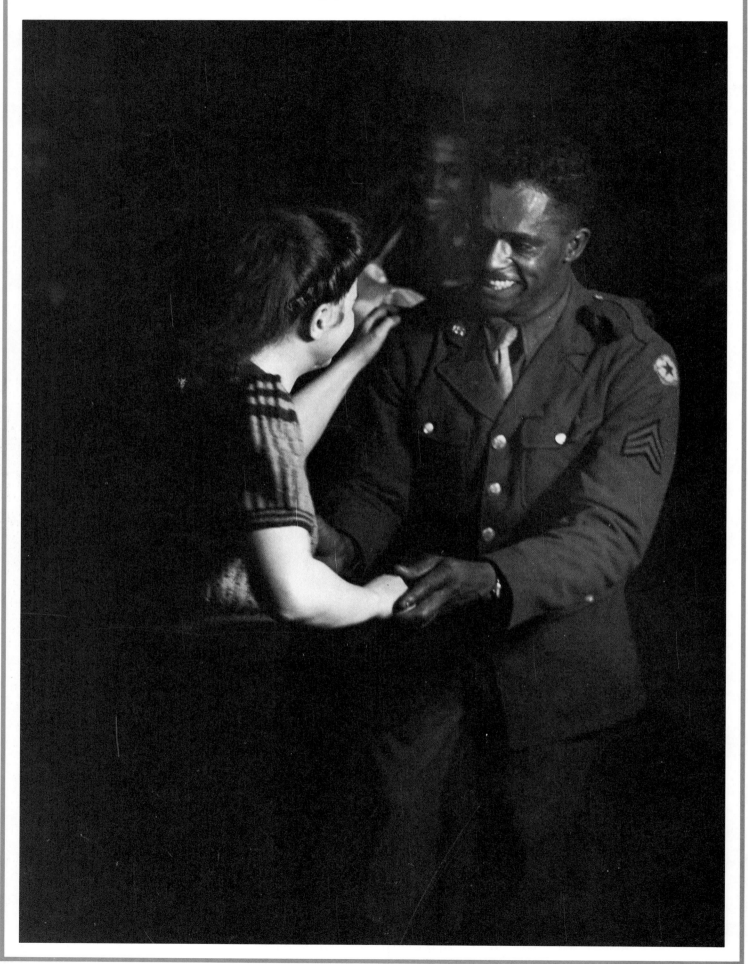

*After the people's war: preparing for the
people's peace; social service centres helping
victims of the bombing in 1944.*

THE NEW JERUSALEM?

1945–1951

O N THE FACES OF THOSE who celebrated the victory in Europe in May 1945 at countless street parties in the towns and villages of the country there is clearly joy, and relief and pride. It was the same kind of knees-up people had, and still have, for coronations, jubilees and royal weddings. But nobody knew then, or learned for certain until late July, what the aspirations of these people were now that the war was over.

In June, the Labour Party held its conference at Blackpool. It was clear that during the war it had won many new adherents. In men like Herbert Morrison, who had responsibility for London during the Blitz, and Ernest Bevin, who also served in the War Cabinet, Labour had experienced and well-known politicians. And the party knew that it was now associated with the promise of major social reform. Clement Attlee, Leader of the Labour Party, encouraged by the exuberance of the conference, pressed for a general election.

Churchill was opposed to this while the war with Japan continued, but, as Labour insisted and as there had been no elections since 1935, he agreed to hold one as soon as was practicable. At the time, not many doubted that the war hero was bound to win. *Picture Post*, however, had taken heed of the Mass Observation opinion poll which suggested otherwise.

Labour won a resounding victory when the results were announced on 26 July. George VI said the result was 'a great surprise to one and all'. The new era was ushered in as Churchill left Buckingham Palace in a chauffeur-driven Rolls Royce having tendered his resignation, and Clement Attlee arrived in a Standard Ten driven by his wife. George VI thought even Attlee looked 'very surprised indeed'.

True to its word, the Labour Government embarked on its ambitious plans: nationalization of the coal mines, railways and, in time, many other key industries; the creation of the National Health Service; a new deal on social security; and a virtual re-building of the cities to provide decent housing for everyone. Full employment would be maintained.

The task was daunting, and, as it turned out, too much to hope for. For vast numbers of people the first opportunity in peacetime for free medical care was a godsend, and affection for the National Health Service never wavered. People had money, too, and work was plentiful. But the country was chronically short of basic materials, of food and clothing. Rationing continued, and the house-building programme was hampered by the shortage of timber.

Britain was, in fact, stony broke. This is not surprising as it had been so since early in the war. It owed £4,198 million according to estimates. It had lost 40 per cent of its overseas trade. The lend-lease arrangement with America was cancelled on 6 August when the atomic bombs dropped on Hiroshima and Nagasaki

VE—Victory in Europe—Day in London in 1945. Hitler was defeated—now the peace was to be won.

brought the war with Japan to an unexpectedly abrupt end.

Yet all the pre-war social problems, apart from unemployment, were still there, and housing was infinitely worse. About a million homes had been wrecked or seriously damaged. In 1948, *Picture Post* visited the Gorbals in Glasgow, where conditions would have shamed a Victorian government.

Between 1945 and 1950 the Government did manage to build 806,000 houses, but they were far too few. Most evocative of this period of austerity is, perhaps, the 'pre-fab'—a prefabricated house which could be assembled quickly on site, often a bomb site. More than 156,000 of these went up, and they proved to be extremely popular with their new occupants. Little gardens were created round them, they had all 'mod cons' inside and many survived long after the emergency conditions for which they were designed. There are still 10,000 intact in the 1990s.

A number of people, desperate for housing, took to squatting. Even the rich were up against it, and the death rattle of the aristocracy was heard once more as they opened the doors of their stately homes to raise money to mend the roof. American tourists arrived on transatlantic liners to take tea with a duke and thrill to the grandeur of his invaded bedchamber.

But the social group who *really* felt they suffered in the immediate post-war years were the middle classes. They were not only still rationed, they were also more heavily taxed. It was estimated that their incomes fell, while those of working people rose. It was the opinion of the novelist Evelyn Waugh that it was impossible for an honest man to save any money between 1940 and 1960.

During the war, rationing had been a great social leveller, and so it continued to be afterwards. Food was a real political issue which boiled over into national protests when powdered egg was reserved for institutions only. Housewives fought back, and hapless Labour politicians were left with powdered egg on their faces. The last straw, as it were, was the introduction of bread rationing—something that had never happened during the war.

The gods were not on the side of the Labour Government, and its popularity began to slip. In 1947, Britain was gripped by one of the coldest winters on record, which produced fuel shortages and a shut-down of factories. Unemployment reached about 800,000 during the freeze.

It was in the following July 1948 that the Health Service came into operation for the first time, after a rearguard action by the British Medical Association, representing family doctors, to oppose it. Quite a number of people celebrated by having all their teeth pulled out and replacing them with a free set of dentures. People who had previously rummaged through stacks of spectacles to find a pair that focused could visit an optician for National Health specs. Women who had paid £6 to a doctor for the delivery of their baby at home, got the service free. But all this cost much more than Labour had bargained for, despite the fact that it was cheap relative to other nations' systems of health care and insurance.

The landscape of British towns, with their smoking chimneys, their Victorian terraces and their bomb sites, were a grim backdrop to the exhortation that in the rapidly changing post-war world Britain could 'make it'. With Germany and Japan temporarily out of action, industry did enjoy a post-war boom, but there was little in the shops as everything was needed for the export drive. Rationing continued into the 1950s, inevitably encouraging the black market and the 'spiv'. In many ways it was just like the war after the Blitz, but without a recognizable enemy.

One result of the fact that people had more money in their pockets but few consumer goods to spend it

Clement Attlee, the first Labour Prime Minister.

A slum in the Gorbals of Glasgow in 1948—a vivid image of the problems the Labour Party tried to tackle.

on was a great surge of enthusiasm for all kinds of entertainment. The late 1940s saw the all-time peak in cinema-going and football crowds. People went out a lot; radio never kept them in in quite the same way that television does today.

There were television programmes, but it was a minority interest. Some people, including *Picture Post*'s soothsayer, thought it would not catch on. Had it remained as it was in the late 1940s, that would probably have been true. It was worthy and educational and closed down in the evenings for an hour so that children could be sent to bed.

It was in this period that the last royal spectacles were staged without stage directions from television. Whereas a Mass Observation poll had found that there was widespread disapproval of a tour undertaken by George VI and the Queen of Southern Africa because it was too expensive, there was much greater enthusiasm for the wedding of Princess Elizabeth and Prince Philip.

It was calculated that the Princess's wedding dress would cost 300 clothing coupons, as rationing stood then, and cost £1,200. The population was divided on whether or not this was too extravagant for the years of austerity. But as the wedding day approached in November 1947 enthusiasm grew, and the section of the population who said they thought it too lavish dropped dramatically. People slept out on pavements to watch the royal procession.

Since the late Victorian period, royalty had been associated in the public mind with Empire. But most knew nothing much about it, except that Britain owned all the bits on the map marked red. By 1947, India had gone, granted a swift and, as it turned out, bloody independence. But Britain still had the greatest Empire the world had ever known, which had fought valiantly for it in the war. A few West Indians had come to Britain as 'Bevin Boys' to work in munitions factories and on airfields when labour was short. Then, in 1947 and 1948, more West Indians arrived on the *Empire Windrush* and other liners.

There had been race riots in sea-port towns in 1919, but it was in the late 1940s that the 'problem' of race relations began to emerge. *Picture Post* carried a story on 'Is There a British Colour Bar?'—a direct reference to circumstances in North America where segregation in the South was institutionalized. Black and white GIs in Britain were subject to an apartheid decreed by General Eisenhower. How would the British react? They muddled along, as always.

For a while, it is said, possession of nuclear weapons (from 1952) compensated for eventual loss of Empire and gave Britain the illusion, at least, of being a world power. But that was not of much concern to the electorate at the end of Labour's first five years in office. Judgement on the New Jerusalem came in the 1950 general election, when the Government's majority was greatly reduced. In 1951 they were dismissed and Churchill was back. It was a decision, as is so often the case in British politics, that had more to do with the eccentric electoral system than a loss of faith in Labour, which got about the same percentage of the vote as in 1945.

In Labour's last years, Britain was at war again—as an ally of the Americans in holding back what was seen as the communist threat to South Korea. There were real fears that another world war would break out, this time between the West and Russia which supported the North Koreans. The war did not have a profound effect on Britain, though it was costly and prices rose. But it was the beginning of the end for *Picture Post* when the proprietor, disillusioned now with the magazine's left-wing stance, dismissed the editor over the disagreement about James Cameron's and Bert Hardy's story on allied mistreatment of communist prisoners.

The New Jerusalem —pre-fabs in Stevenage, 1953.

An austerity bright spot: Princess Elizabeth's wedding in 1947.

A small boy stays up to listen to the radio, 1947.

THE NEW JERUSALEM?

The hopes for a better post-war world are captured in these pictures as the war ended: a soldier returning home to a pre-fab (opposite); and celebrations of VE day (above and below). Things did get better, but there was much disillusionment as well.

THE NEW JERUSALEM?

Some of the builders of Britain's brand-new Welfare State, gathering for Labour's conference just after the end of the war in Europe (opposite below). They decided to fight an election as soon as possible. Among the old guard of trades unionists (opposite top) and politicians—Clement Attlee (right) and Herbert Morrison, with Barbara Castle (below)—there were new faces, such as that of Major Denis Healey (bottom). For the first time in history, the Labour Party sensed it could take a firm hold on the reins of government.

THE NEW JERUSALEM?

Few believed that the British electorate would reject the great war hero Churchill in the 1945 election. But the groundswell of support for social reform had grown at the end of the war, and, as it turned out, new leaders were chosen to win the peace. Picture Post's story 'The Nation Considers its Verdict' showed Ernest Bevin canvassing in Wandsworth (right), *a Conservative peer, Lord Buckhurst, in Bethnal Green* (below)—*and the lively reaction of one of the canvassed* (opposite).

The new Labour Government embarked upon its widely supported programme of social reforms when the nation was effectively bankrupt and a great many problems had been aggravated by the war. The popular priority for the New Jerusalem was better housing. Many people were squatting, some in the New Forest (left); others lived in Victorian slums (below); but there was a shortage of materials and of funds to build new homes (opposite above). A bathroom was a great symbol of social advancement in the immediate post-war years, though many people managed to make themselves very comfortable in the most unfavourable circumstances: a well-stocked back garden in Hoxton, East London in 1946 (opposite below).

(Overleaf) *A basement flat in the Elephant and Castle, south London, in 1939.*

THE NEW JERUSALEM?

After the Second World War, as after the First, the death rattle of Britain's upper crust was heard throughout the land. But wealth survived. Maybe they had never had it so bad, but reports of the death of status and privilege were exaggerated. As time went on, the egalitarian mood that had prevailed during the war began to disappear as former attitudes reasserted themselves.

A shock to British sensibilities—the arrival of Americans on ocean liners who just loved to visit ailing stately homes and boost restoration funds.

The continuation of rationing after the war probably helped the poor but the over-taxed middle classes protested. 'Is the Middle Class Doomed?' asked Picture Post.

The bitter winter of 1947 threw people out of work, tramline points froze and it took pneumatic drills to dig up parsnips.

The first days of the National Health Service and the Welfare State—however much they fell short of the ideal—fulfilled the dreams of many. Especially the free spectacles.

The reality, and the dream, of the years of austerity. Warren Street, London, in 1949 (opposite) *and images from the 1946 'Britain Can Make It' Exhibition, which was ahead of its time in its modernism* (above and below).

*A characteristic figure of the years of rationing was the 'spiv'—
a Flash Harry who made a dubious living selling mysteriously
acquired goods. Because rationing survived the end of the war by a
decade, so did the spivs, wonderfully depicted in this 1946 feature
from* Picture Post *on London's so-called Loot Alley. In a sense,
the free market was reasserting itself after the wartime controls—
the spiv was to become a rare species in the affluent Fifties.*

The late *1940s* were the peak years for all kinds of public entertainment, from drinking in pubs to watching football. It was a time before television became widespread, and when people had money in their pockets but few goods to spend it on. So the modest wealth of the demobbed soldier and the factory worker tended to go on cinema tickets, beer and football: crowds at Ibrox Park, Glasgow (above and right) *and* Wolverhampton (below), *in 1949*. Entertainment was still more public than it was to become in the relatively affluent Fifties.

Though there had been race riots in some seaports in 1919, colour was not much of an issue in Britain until after the war. West Indians, many of whom had served in the British forces, began to arrive in 1948 in search of work. Attentive as ever to social trends, Picture Post *was asking in* 1949: 'Is There a British Colour Bar?' *Practically nothing was done by officialdom to acknowledge the arrival of Indians or West Indians, or to help them settle in.*

THE NEW JERUSALEM?

*The beginning of the end of Labour's New Jerusalem—
canvassing for the 1950 General Election which they
narrowly won. By the following year they had lost power.*

YOU'VE NEVER HAD IT SO GOOD

1951–1957

Looking back, it is possible to say that the turning point for the country, the shift from austerity to a new spirit of unidealistic consumerism, was the staging of the Festival of Britain from May to September 1951. The cynics asked what there was to celebrate, and several times in the planning stages the Festival came close to being abandoned. What had begun as a proposal by the Royal Society of Arts back in 1943 (for a grandiose replica of the celebrated Crystal Palace Exhibition in Hyde Park in 1851, at the height of Britain's industrial power) became a much more modest affair, lashed together. It was, in a sense, Labour's swan song by the Thames.

As the humorist and playwright Michael Frayn put it, the Festival was 'the last and virtually posthumous work of the Herbivore Britain of the BBC News, the Crown Film Unit, the sweet ration, the Ealing comedies, Uncle Mac, Sylvia Peters . . . all the great fixed stars by which my childhood was navigated'. By 'Herbivore', Frayn meant those worthies who still had a social conscience, in contrast to 'Carnivores' like the novelist Evelyn Waugh who hated the Festival.

Eight million people visited the Festival and the adjoining pleasure gardens in Battersea Park. They wondered at the Dome of Discovery, and enjoyed the joke about the strange Skylon structure—like Britain, it had no visible means of support. They danced in the open air and enjoyed themselves. They were 'giving themselves a pat on the back', according to the Labour Minister Herbert Morrison. It was a populist event, devised by a highbrow Festival committee, of which the architect Hugh Casson was a member. He recalled later for a BBC TV series, *Now the War is Over*:

> 'We all had, I suppose, in a way, rather naive views that England could be better and was going to be better—that the arts and architecture and music and healthy air and Jaeger underwear and all these things, which the garden city movement stood for, were in fact the keys to some sort of vague Utopia.'

The people voted for the Festival with their feet, but voted Labour out with their ballot papers. When the Conservatives returned to power they got rid of nearly all of it—only the Festival Hall, intended as a permanent fixture, remains. For many years the ruins of the Festival pavilions were used as car parks.

Rationing began to disappear, although some lingered on until 1956. And then a new Elizabethan era was ushered in. King George VI, everyone knew, had been ill, but they thought he was getting

Harold Macmillan, later known as 'Supermac', coined the phrase: 'Let's face it, most of us have never had it so good.'

better, and news of his death on 6 February 1952 was a shock—recorded in detail, once again, by Mass Observation.

Thousands queued all night to file past the coffin in Westminster Hall, and many thousands more lined the route of the funeral procession. Mass Observation observers and diarists reported people standing to attention in their homes when the national anthem came on the radio. There was sympathy for the once reluctant monarch who had done 'a good job' and for the young Princess Elizabeth who, at the age of only 26, was about to become Queen.

Nobody really anticipated what a spectacular success the Coronation of June 1953 would be. As with Princess Elizabeth's wedding, the tapping of public opinion showed a crescendo of enthusiasm. People worried less about the cost of it all. 'The bigger the show the better. It will bring lots of Americans with their dollars,' was a comment made to Mass Observation.

There were street parties throughout the country, and the shops and houses of many streets were hung with patriotic bunting. This was the first royal event to get a mass television audience, and really marked the start of television as a powerful force in the nation. Many people packed picnics and went to join friends and relations who had a television to make a day of it. Those who slept all night to get a good vantage point on the route had to endure a miserable rainy day. But the weather did not deter the party-goers.

Here was the nation, only a couple of years after the demise of the brave new world of the first-ever Labour government, celebrating a new Elizabethan Age.

These were the early years of what was to be called the 'consumer society', as the home was transformed by a range of gadgetry which today is familiar to nearly everyone. In 1956, only eight per cent of homes had refrigerators. To have a telephone or a motor car was unusual—car workers *cycled* to the factory, or they walked. But the signs of a new affluence were there, and theorists began to write of the *embourgeoisement* of the working classes whose modest prosperity was encouraging them to adopt the values of the middle classes. In the 1950s, wealth was personified in the lavish lifestyle of Lord and Lady Docker, on whom *Picture Post* expended an entire feature.

It was a measure of rising standards of living that more people got longer holidays. The English seaside resorts, creations of the Victorian and Edwardian age, enjoyed their last great boom before the package holiday made them look out-of-date, although already in the 1950s a new kind of coach party could be found leaving for the not-so-grand tour of Spain or Italy. And the holiday camp, invented in the 1930s, had an enormous following, providing at an all-in price board, lodging and entertainment. By the 1950s they were more 'down-market' than in the 1940s, when middle-class holidaymakers could still be found at Butlins. During the war, Billy Butlin had handed over his camps to the military, and in the egalitarian mood of the post-war years social classes mixed in them. It was a sign of the reassertion of social class divisions that this was much less true in the Fifties.

An entirely new group of 'consumers' made a flamboyant appearance in the Fifties: youth. Young people in work, but living at home, got a more than proportionate share of the affluence of the Fifties and Sixties. They spent their high 'disposable incomes' on clothes and music. Teddy boys—a kind of joke version of the Edwardian swell—were the most conspicuous, and for the older generation, the most worrying group. Outlandish teenage fashion is very familiar now, but it was not then. The film *Rock Around the Clock* with Bill Haley arrived from America in 1956, and was a landmark of youth culture.

Much American popular culture had arrived with the GIs stationed in Britain during the war. Jazz was very exciting then, its derivation from black music

The lying-in-State at Westminster of George VI in 1952.

A new voice for the Fifties, Brendan Behan.

still risqué. Home-grown popular music was in its infancy, and what was then regarded as shockingly innovative is now charmingly quaint: the Liberace Fan Club, for example. John Lennon and Paul McCartney were playing with the Quarrymen in Liverpool in 1956.

'Modern Art' was also a topic guaranteed to provoke outrage, with Abstraction, whether in painting or sculpture, providing an easy comic target. Fashion, however, became more rational and accessible: mass-produced clothing, once rationing had gone, allowed women to look 'smart' cheaply.

Because there were so few cars on the roads the streets were relatively free of traffic. It is startling to see now the photographs published in *Picture Post* in the mid-1950s of whole areas with hardly a car on the road. The street was the only playground for many children, a matter for social concern at the time.

So too was pollution—from chimneys, not exhaust fumes. Young people born after the 1960s tend to disbelieve the degree to which cities were blackened with soot. The first experiments in cleaning up the atmosphere were made in Manchester in 1954. It was an enormous task, replacing coal fires with electric and gas or insisting on smokeless fuel. The Clean Air Act was passed in 1956, and the last great London smog was in the winter of 1962–63.

Unemployment remained very low in the 1950s, but there was still a flow of emigrants from Britain, mostly to Australia and Canada, some to South Africa, seeking their fortune. In 1952–53 more people left Britain than arrived from overseas. This was reversed in the mid-1950s. Often encouraged to seek work in sectors of industry which were short of labour, more West Indians arrived in this period. Whereas in the late Forties practically nothing had been done to assist immigrants, an effort was now made to greet those arriving from abroad. No reliable figures were kept on immigration at this time, but later estimates suggest that in the early 1950s the Indians were the largest 'coloured' group, followed by the West Indians, thought to number over 15,000 in 1951. There were communities from Cyprus and, from outside the Empire, Italy. Britain was becoming conscious of itself as a multi-racial society.

Britain still imagined it had a world role, though in terms of industrial and military power it had been eclipsed by America and Russia. This hubris brought it to embark on a disastrous assault on Egypt, together with the French, to reclaim the Suez canal after it had been nationalized by President Nasser. America, then avowedly anti-Imperialist, would not back the operation, and Britian had to make an ignominious withdrawal.

It was a peculiar and contradictory time. Beneath the surface prosperity celebrated in Macmillan's dictum, 'Let's face it, most of us have never had it so good,' there was a great deal of social tension. There was a consciousness that the economic boom was in some way false, based as it was on American loans and the weak state of rivals in Europe and Japan in the first years after the war. And there was frustration with lingering Victorianism, which burst out in literature and theatre with the so-called Angry Young Men (all of whom became less radical in time). They were principally John Braine, Kingsley Amis and, perhaps most celebrated of all at the time, the playwright John Osborne. He was a local newspaper journalist, 27 years old when he wrote *Look Back in Anger*. It was first performed in 1956.

This was the beginning of a moral stylistic revolt which flowered in the Sixties. What was terribly modern then now looks like a museum piece. It was all anti-Victorian, sparse, uncluttered. Within a few years the Beatles were world-famous; but that was in the 'Swinging Sixties', long after *Picture Post* had gone and after the era in British history of which it was so evocative had also come to an end.

War work over: women as car 'salesmen'.   *A jig for the affluent Fifties: holiday camp, 1953.*

An historical turning point: the evocative Festival of Britain held on the South Bank of the Thames in 1951. It was the creation of an educated, liberal intellectual set, and dismissed by some as a silly socialist extravaganza at a time of economic hardship. But it turned out to be very popular. 'The British giving themselves a pat on the back,' said Herbert Morrison, the Labour Minister behind the event.

(Overleaf) Goodbye austerity: a cheerful trio at the funfair in Battersea Park, a popular attraction of the Festival of Britain.

Rationing was not lifted until a long time after the end of the war. In fact, new forms of rationing—of bread, for a time—were introduced in the late 1940s. When the ration books finally began to disappear in the Fifties there were impromptu celebrations—sweets came off in 1953, and so did meat. The era of imported powdered egg, of whalemeat and the strange tinned fish, snoek, was over.

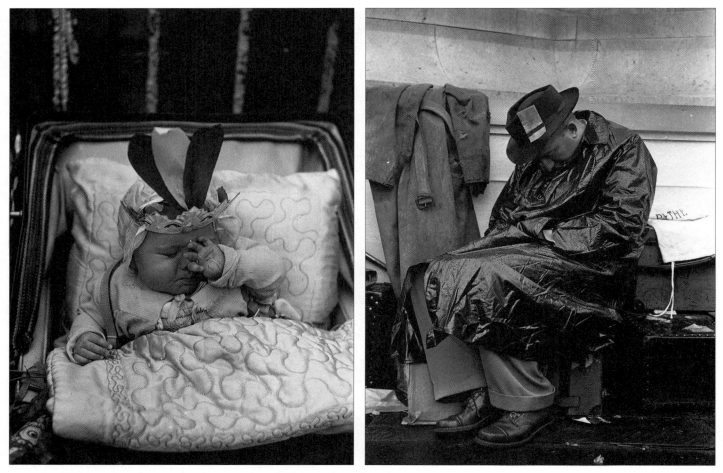

The dawn of the new Elizabethan era on a rainy June day in 1953, greeted more enthusiastically by some than others . . .

YOU'VE NEVER HAD IT SO GOOD

Coronation street parties were held all over the country. But none celebrated more exuberantly than London's East Enders who had a Picture Post feature to themselves. After Britain's brief flirtation, during and just after the war, with a kind of socialism, the traditional values of patriotism and love of royalty were reasserting themselves in the 1950s. Many people saved for months to pay for their street parties, which went on well into the night.

The first mass television audience in Britain was for the Coronation in 1953. Then, in 1955, Independent Television arrived and stole the ratings. It was the dawn of the television age. Noddy was one of the first stars of ITV (right). By 1951 Picture Post *realized it had a rival in the* BBC (below). *1955:* Café Continental (opposite below) *and a game show* (opposite above).

(Overleaf) *A poignant image from* 1952. *A jovial cotton worker with telly, but this Lancashire industry was in sharp decline.*

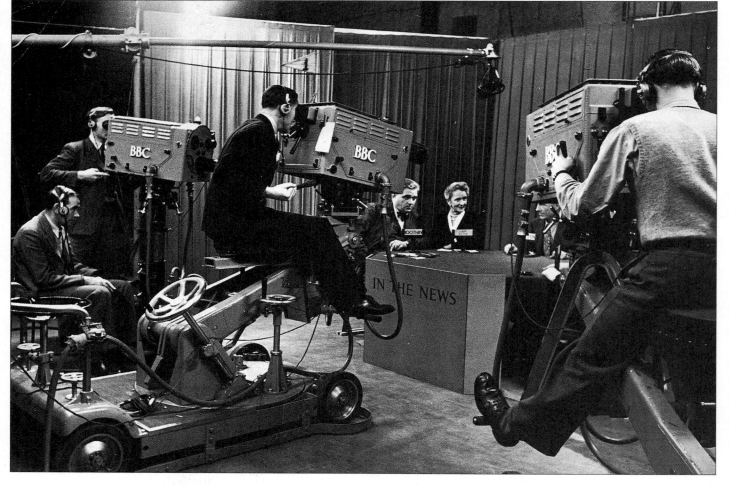

YOU'VE NEVER HAD IT SO GOOD

*The quaint old modernity of the 1950s: formica, and
snack bars, self-service supermarkets, frozen foods
and the launderette. It was a brave new world and
a final rejection of the customs of Victorian England.
A profound change in the lives of many people
was ushered in.*

The epitome of garish Fifties opulence—the much-publicized and often reviled lifestyle of Lord and Lady Docker (above and below). One of their showpieces of conspicuous consumption was a gold Daimler. This kind of showing-off was hardly acceptable during the war and the years of austerity. (Opposite) *The Cabaret Club around 1957.*

The start of the era of the cheap package holiday abroad. A trip to Italy by coach in *1951* (left and bottom), *exposing white English skin to the relentless sun of Assisi. The more adventurous hitchhiked: two English girls travelled to the Riviera on £5* (below). *By the mid-1950s a new kind of English culinary imperialism was spreading across the Channel.* (Opposite) *Boulogne 1955—*pommes frites *with everything and a chef who had perhaps stayed on after D-Day.*

Before holidays abroad and cheap charter flights, the English seaside resorts and holiday camps enjoyed a last great era. A sun-tan was still quite a rare status symbol. Most people who got a holiday braved the British weather. August on Scarborough beach, 1952 (left); romancing Butlins Redcoats in 1953, Des O'Connor and his wife Phyllis Gill (below left); Southend, 1952 (below right); knobbly knees on parade at Butlins, 1953 (opposite).

An entirely new
youth culture,
greatly influenced by
America, emerged in
the 1950s, drumming
out the Victorian era
of which many
aspects had survived
the first half of the
twentieth century.
Jazz, first, and then
pop music swept
across the country.
Rock 'n' roll and the
Teddy Boy symbol-
ized the new era.

(Overleaf) *Teds
looking cool in 1956.*

LIPCHITZ

Modern art in the Fifties was generally the subject of ridicule or downright disgust. (Opposite) Comedian Max Bygraves muses over a Battersea Park sculpture at the time of the Festival of Britain. (Above) Schoolboys trying to figure out the meaning of a piece of wood; and (below) a startled lady at the Tate Gallery photographed in 1957.

PICTURE POST BRITAIN

Contrasting Fifties fashions. The bra and corset are not yet discarded, but there is the beginning of a loosening-up of style, as the young stop aspiring to haute couture *and start wearing jeans.*

After the war, women had to find their place again, in the office, in industry and in social life. Some contrasting images of the older and younger generation. (Opposite above) *Whitehall charladies objecting to a farthing (one quarter of an old penny) rise offered by the Treasury in 1951.* (Opposite below) *The 'Fluffers' working to clean up the Underground in London at night after the electricity has been switched off. Some switched-on Fifties girls: a night club hostess* (above); *Windmill girls sunning themselves* (below); *and a smart shop assistant* (right).

The task of rebuilding Britain's crumbling Victorian cities had hardly begun in the Fifties. The motor car had not yet come to dominate the streets which were the playground for most children in towns. The planners were only just beginning to get to work. In 1954 Picture Post *agonized over the death of children on the roads and the rise in juvenile crime, especially in London. Thurston Hopkins took the pictures for their 'Children of the Streets' feature* (below, bottom left and right). (Right) Liverpool in 1957, *and the plans to transform it* (opposite below).

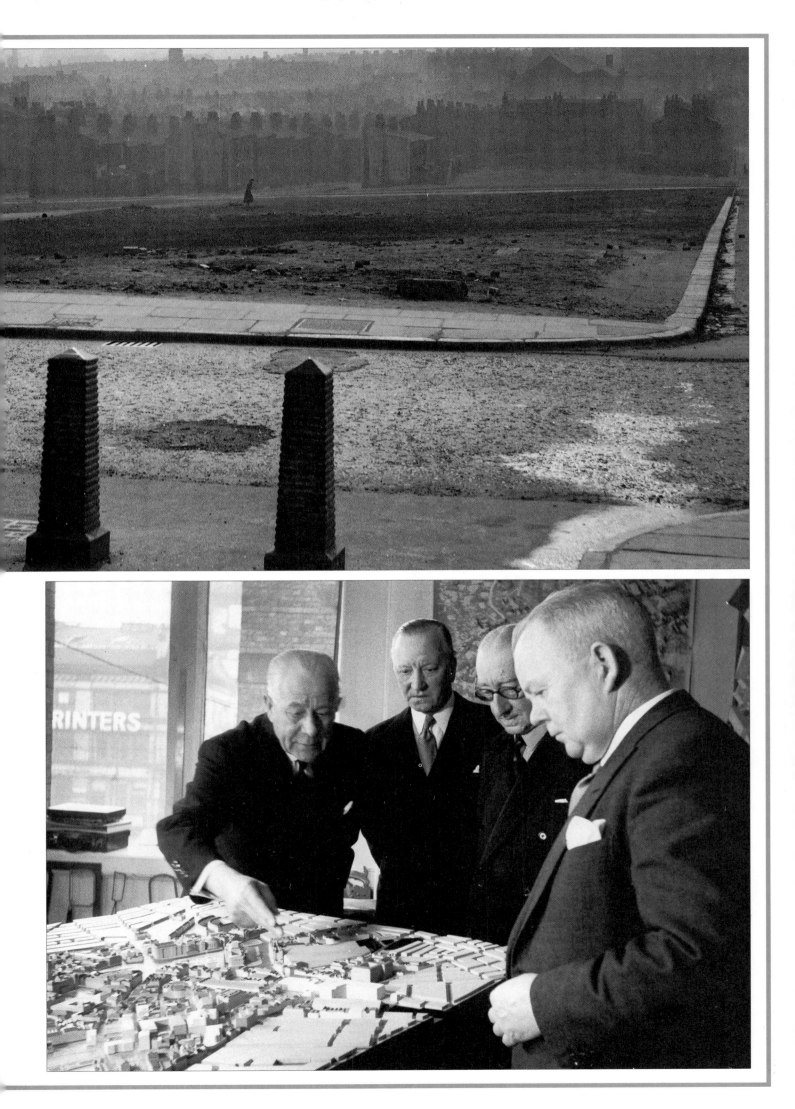

Smog—the environmental nightmare of the Victorian age which blackened and choked cities until the 1960s. The mammoth task of getting rid of it began in the 1950s. It meant outlawing the use of coal in domestic fires and in industry, and paying compensation to those who had to switch to smokeless fuel, gas or electricity. The Clean Air Act was passed in 1956, and bit by bit the country became brighter. But it was not until the Sixties that the Act really had a noticeable effect. Smog is now a part of history.

Leaving and arriving. Emigration to Commonwealth countries—Canada, Australia and New Zealand—was still a popular way of seeking a better standard of living in the 1950s. So was immigration to Britain from other parts of the Commonwealth. For the young, departure and arrival were hard. (Above) A sad leaving of Liverpool for this girl on her way to Canada in 1955; (opposite) a weary West Indian girl at Victoria Station at the end of her journey via Southampton to London.

The Suez crisis of 1956: a Royal Variety show is cancelled, people queue for petrol coupons, and a protester lobbies Whitehall.

Look Back in Anger, *by Angry Young Man John Osborne, first staged at the Royal Court Theatre in 1956.*

Jiving, and just sitting around drinking coffee and smoking in the mid-1950s. A new generation that did not know about the war had been brought up in the Welfare State—and had no Picture Post *to fire its imagination about the world.*

The television age spelt the end for Picture
Post *magazine. It had stood at one time for
ideals and a new Britain, but ceased
publication at the dawn of the age of
affluence. Britain was becoming stylish, a
forerunner of the Sixties, with pioneers like
Shirley and Terence Conran (below). It was
not long before nearly every home had a
television, and a wonder of the age—colour
TV—was spoken of.*

ACKNOWLEDGEMENTS

The pictures in this book all come from the Hulton Picture Company. The majority of photographs were taken by the staff photographers at Picture Post; these fall into several categories— pictures published in the magazine, overs and photographs taken for stories that were never used. We have tried to identify the work of individual photographers, but in some cases it is difficult to be certain as several photographers covered the same story.

In addition there are photographs from the four major agencies which supplied Picture Post with material. Some, though not all, of the ones in this book were published in the magazine.

The publishers would like to thank the staff of the Hulton Picture Company for their valuable help in compiling this collection.

Picture Post: Maurice Ambler 90, 132 (centre); Hans Bauman (known as Felix Mann) 13 (bottom left), 14 (bottom), 48, 49, 52, 53, 54 (bottom right), 71 (top left); Bill Brandt 6 (below left), 7 (below right), 21, 67, 78 (bottom right), 86 (bottom); John Chillingworth 8 (bottom left), 105 (top and bottom right), 120, 122, 123, 126/7, 128 (centre and bottom); 142 (top left and right), 153; Augustus Darwell 22/3, 30, 31 (bottom right); Alex Dellow 125 (top), 136, 138/9, 146 (top), 147, 148 (bottom right), 150, 159; Gerti Deutsch 2; George Douglas 119 (bottom), 129; Jack Esten 9 (bottom right); Tim Gidal 7 (bottom left), 16; Zoltan Glass 54 (left); Bert Hardy 6 (bottom left), 7 (bottom right), 8 (centre and right), 40 (top left), 43, 46 (top right), 47, 54 (top right), 58, 59, 62, 63, 78 (centre), 79 (right), 86, 88/9, 91, 92, 96 (bottom), 98, 104, 106 (bottom), 107, 108, 109, 113 (right), 130, 131, 134 (bottom left and right), 135, 142 (top left), 144 (top), 145 (bottom left), 159; Charles Hewitt 9 (left), 87, 100, 105 (bottom left), 109, 113 (left), 128 (top), 133 (bottom), 137 (top), 140, 145 (bottom right), 154, 155; Thurston Hopkins 106 (top), 122, 123, 124 (top), 125 (bottom), 133 (top), 134 (top), 146 (centre, bottom left and right), 156; Kurt Hubschmann (known as Kurt Hutton) 12 (bottom right), 16, 20, 24, 25, 26, 27, 31, 38 (bottom left), 57, 69, 70, 71 (right), 73, 74, 75, 82, 83, 84, 94, 95 (bottom), 98 (bottom), 104 (bottom); Raymond Kleboe 101, 141 (top), 148 (bottom right), 157; Leonard McCombe 38 (centre), 39, 40 (bottom), 46 (top left), 52, 53, 66; Joseph McKeown 132, 137 (bottom), 145 (top), 158; Haywood Magee 1, 6 (right), 38 (right), 40 (bottom), 46 (top left), 51 (top right), 52, 53, 60, 61, 62/3, 65 (bottom), 76/7, 78 (right), 81, 84, 85, 93, 99, 105, 110, 112 (centre), 116/7, 124 (bottom), 151; John Murray 131; Francis Reiss 76/7, 81, 87 (bottom); Grace Robertson 118, 119, 141 (bottom); Humphrey Spender 13 (right), 18, 19, 35 (top), 64, 65; Ronald Startup 120 (top right and bottom); Carl Sutton 143.
Central Press: 29, 79 (bottom left), 121;
Fox 10, 14 (top), 15, 28, 33, 36, 42 (top), 45, 46 (bottom), 50, 51 (bottom), 68, 71 (centre left), 80;
Keystone 17, 35 (bottom), 40 (top right), 41, 45 (bottom), 55, 71 (bottom left), 97, 102/3;
Topical 12 (bottom left), 29 (bottom), 31 (top), 32, 44, 51 (top left), 56, 96 (top), 144 (bottom), 149, 152.

Extracts from Mass Observation reports are reproduced by kind permission of the Mass Observation Archive.